MENSA®
MIND
PUZZLES™

MENSA®
MIND
PUZZLES™

100 WORD AND LOGIC GAMES TO IMPROVE YOUR MEMORY, SHARPEN YOUR WIT, AND TRAIN YOUR BRAIN

DAVID MILLAR

Skyhorse Publishing

Copyright © 2018 by Skyhorse Publishing

All rights reserved. No part of this book may be reproduced in any manner without the express written consent of the publisher, except in the case of brief excerpts in critical reviews or articles. All inquiries should be addressed to Skyhorse Publishing, 307 West 36th Street, 11th Floor, New York, NY 10018.

Skyhorse Publishing books may be purchased in bulk at special discounts for sales promotion, corporate gifts, fund-raising, or educational purposes. Special editions can also be created to specifications. For details, contact the Special Sales Department, Skyhorse Publishing, 307 West 36th Street, 11th Floor, New York, NY 10018 or info@skyhorsepublishing.com.

Skyhorse® and Skyhorse Publishing® are registered trademarks of Skyhorse Publishing, Inc.®, a Delaware corporation.

Visit our website at www.skyhorsepublishing.com.

10 9 8 7 6 5 4 3

Library of Congress Cataloging-in-Publication Data is available on file.

Cover design by Brian Peterson
Cover illustration by David Millar

ISBN: 978-1-5107-3863-8

Printed in China

CONTENTS

PUZZLES

Maze 1

In this maze, you may cross under paths using
tunnels where indicated by arrows.

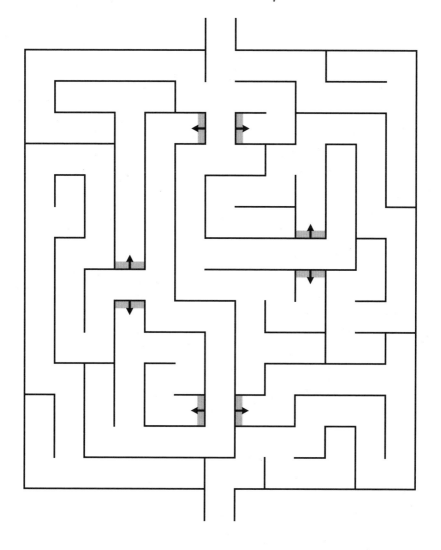

Story Logic 1

Time for a coffee run! Use the clues provided to figure out the orders for four friends so they each get the right flavor and size, as well as how much they each owe for their drink.

		Size				Price				Flavor			
		Small	Medium	Large	Extra Large	$1.25	$1.75	$2.25	$3.25	Caramel	Donut Shop	Eclair	Fudge
Friend	Miley												
	Nupur												
	Ozie												
	Paige												
Flavor	Caramel												
	Donut Shop												
	Eclair												
	Fudge												
Price	$1.25												
	$1.75												
	$2.25												
	$3.25												

Paige's drink was larger than the drink that cost $1.25.

The donut shop blend was a larger size than Miley's drink, but smaller than the caramel coffee drink.

The eclair flavored coffee drink cost more than the caramel coffee drink.

The extra large drink did not cost $1.75.

Nupur was the one who ordered donut shop blend.

The fudge-flavored coffee drink cost exactly $1.00 more than the drink in the small cup.

Ozie, who ordered either caramel or fudge coffee, paid $3.25 for her drink.

Numcross 1

Use the provided clues to fill the grid with numbers.
No entry may start with a 0.

A	B	C		D	E
F			■	G	
■		H	I		
J	K			■	■
L		■	M	N	O
P		■	Q		

Across

A.   3 × Q across
D.   2 × O down
F.   3 × D down
G.   O down in reverse
H.   Prince song
J.   Smashing Pumpkins song
L.   H across - J across
M.   G across squared
P.   One-half of L across
Q.   Consecutive digits in ascending order

Down

A.   G across + 6
B.   N down - 1
C.   (10 × K down) + F across
D.   Digits that sum to 14
E.   Wrestler Rey Mysterio's signature move
I.   H across in reverse
J.   A perfect square
K.   Skateboarder Tony Hawk's signature move
N.   2 × G across
O.   P across + 3

Symbol Sums 1

The sums of five combinations of symbols have been provided. What is the value of each individual symbol?

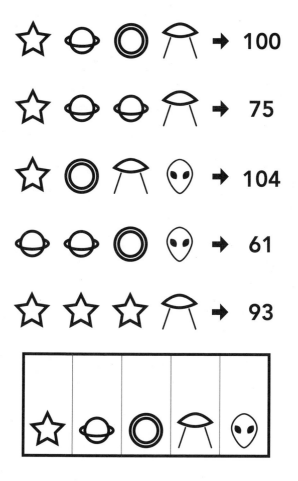

Cube Logic 1

Which of the four foldable patterns can be folded to
make the cube displayed?

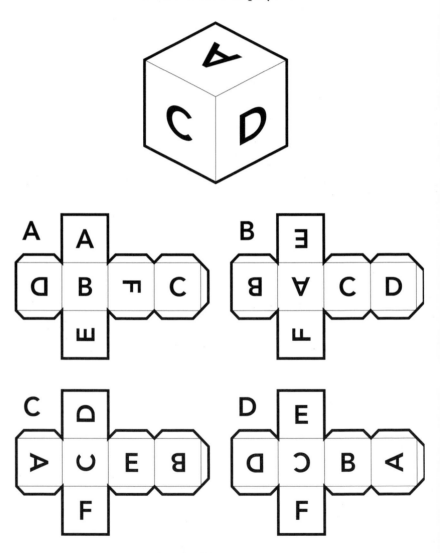

Pent Words 1

Split the grid into shapes, and use the clues provided to spell five-letter words across each row and within each shape. Shape clues include an outline, but the shape may be rotated or reflected.

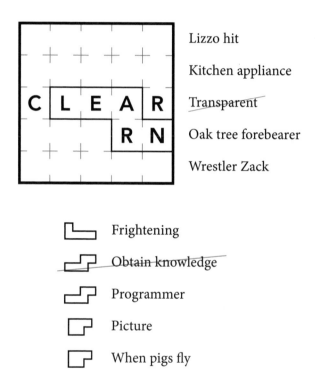

Lizzo hit

Kitchen appliance

Transparent

Oak tree forebearer

Wrestler Zack

Frightening

Obtain knowledge

Programmer

Picture

When pigs fly

Two words have been completed to get you started!

Rearrangement 1–2

Rearrange the letters in the phrase "BRACED DELIS" to spell something sandwich shops need to prepare for the lunch rush.

Rearrange the letters in the phrase "HE HOGGED THE COINS" to spell a video game character that was actually more into rings than coins.

Black Holes 1

Divide the grid into chunks along the guides
provided so that each chunk contains one black
hole, and so the digits in the chunk sum to the
number in the black hole.

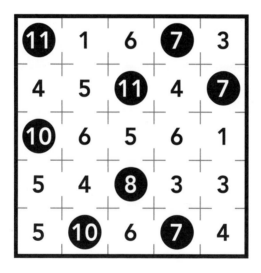

Word Sudoku 1

In the sudoku grid, enter one of each of six unique letters into each row, column, and boldly-outlined six-celled rectangle without repetition.

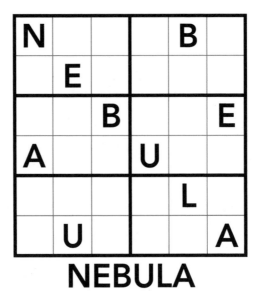

NEBULA

Ringed Planet 1

Use the clues to place six words, each six letters in length, around the planet. Words may go clockwise or counterclockwise as needed.

Drained

Italian Subgroup

Keep

Missing

Moistened

Waivering

Tetra Grid 1

Drop each of the shapes and their letters into the grid to spell ten six-letter words. Clues for the words have been provided next to the grid.

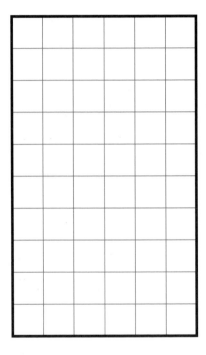

'fraidy cat

Leisurely

Car storage place

Like some Nordic seafarers

Camera accessory

Constituents

Tall tale

Rubber ball activity

Permeable

Like some old films

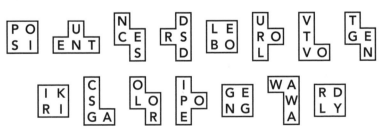

Symbol Sums 2

The sums of five combinations of symbols have been provided. What is the value of each individual symbol?

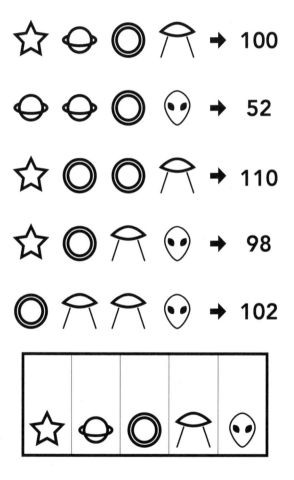

Maze 2

In this maze, you may cross under paths using tunnels where indicated by arrows.

Numcross 2

Use the provided clues to fill the grid with numbers.
No entry may start with a 0.

A	B		C	D	E
F			G		
H		I			
		J		K	L
M	N			O	
P				Q	

Across

A. Number of ounces in one pound

C. A palindrome

F. A across - 3

G. F across × M down

H. Year when the Obama presidency concluded

J. H across × 3

M. G across - 6

O. A perfect square

P. M across - N down

Q. Number of fluid ounces in one quart

Down

A. L down - N down

B. Digits that sum to 9

C. Digits that sum to 18

D. O across - 1

E. 2 × D down

I. P across × 8

K. Consecutive digits in descending order

L. 2 × E down

M. Q across - 10

N. A across × 5

Story Logic 2

Lots of goods are on offer at the local mercantile and antique market. Use the clues and map provided to match the vendor name with their booth number and how much you spent there.

		Vendor Name						Money Spent					
		Brooks Leather	Chimes by Linda	Knasty Knits	Lee's Lotions	Misremembered Things	Sandworks	$5	$10	$15	$20	$30	$40
Booth Number	103												
	104												
	105												
	106												
	107												
	108												
Money Spent	$5												
	$10												
	$15												
	$20												
	$30												
	$40												

More was spent at Lee's Lotions than at Knasty Knits.

More was spent at booth 106 than at booths 104 and 107 combined.

Sandworks is located directly between Knasty Knits and Brooks Leather.

$30 was spent at booth 108, which is more than the amount spent at the booth directly across the hall.

Chimes by Linda is not in booth 106.

The goods from booth 105 cost twice as much as those from booth 103.

Lee's Lotions, which is in booth 107, shares a wall with Misremembered Things.

Twice as much was spent at Misremembered Things than at the booth directly across the hall from it.

106	107	108	109
105	104	103	102

Pent Words 2

Split the grid into shapes, and use the clues provided to spell five-letter words across each row and within each shape. Shape clues include an outline, but the shape may be rotated or reflected.

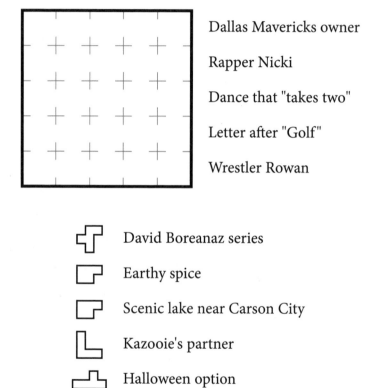

Dallas Mavericks owner

Rapper Nicki

Dance that "takes two"

Letter after "Golf"

Wrestler Rowan

David Boreanaz series

Earthy spice

Scenic lake near Carson City

Kazooie's partner

Halloween option

Word Sudoku 2

In the sudoku grid, enter one of each of six unique letters into each row, column, and boldly-outlined six-celled rectangle without repetition.

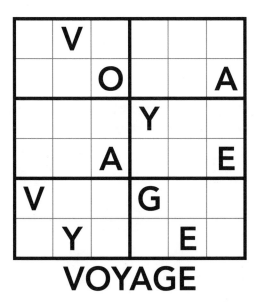

VOYAGE

Black Holes 2

Divide the grid into chunks along the guides provided so that each chunk contains one black hole, and so the digits in the chunk sum to the number in the black hole.

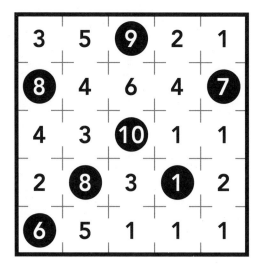

Maze 3

In this maze, you may cross under paths using
tunnels where indicated by arrows.

Ringed Planet 2

Use the clues to place six words, each six letters in
length, around the planet. Words may go clockwise
or counterclockwise as needed.

Activity

Destroyed with Fire

DIYer: ___ it!

Noises

Removed

Ruined Grape

Tetra Grid 2

Drop each of the shapes and their letters into the grid to spell ten six-letter words. Clues for the words have been provided next to the grid.

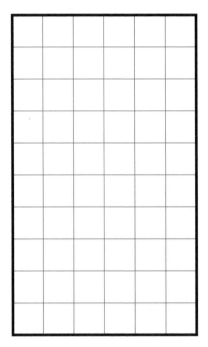

Sundae topper

Hot season

Best day of the work week

Vampire deterrant

"Wanted" poster feature

Scared

Invigorate

Gym item

Office supply item

Couch potato's device

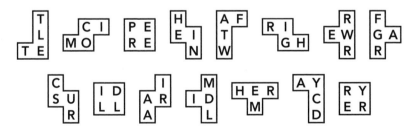

Rearrangement 3–4

Rearrange the letters in the phrase "CHAPS LIKE" to spell a snack that old chaps of the vegan persuasion are really into.

Rearrange the letters in the phrase "GO FEEL GOURMET" to spell a really big breakfast.

Cube Logic 2

Which of the four foldable patterns can be folded to make the cube displayed?

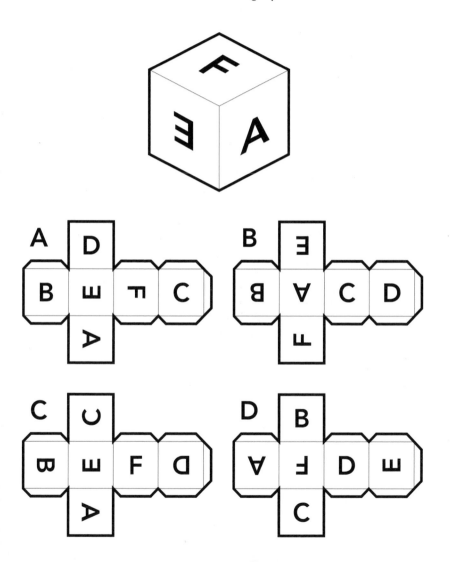

Word Sudoku 3

In the sudoku grid, enter one of each of six unique letters into each row, column, and boldly-outlined six-celled rectangle without repetition.

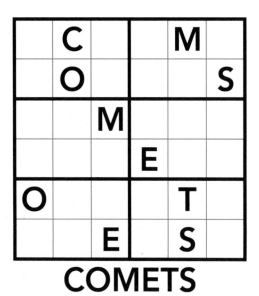

COMETS

Pent Words 3

Split the grid into shapes, and use the clues provided to spell five-letter words across each row and within each shape. Shape clues include an outline, but the shape may be rotated or reflected.

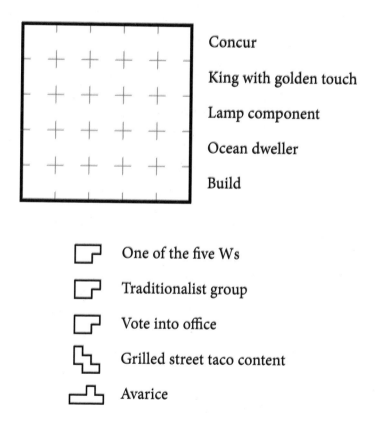

Concur

King with golden touch

Lamp component

Ocean dweller

Build

One of the five Ws

Traditionalist group

Vote into office

Grilled street taco content

Avarice

Numcross 3

Use the provided clues to fill the grid with numbers.
No entry may start with a 0.

A	B	C		D	E
F				G	
		H	I		
J	K				
L			M	N	O
P			Q		

Across

A. D across × L across

D. P across - 7

F. O down + Q across

G. One-fifth of Q across

H. A multiple of O down

J. I down + F across

L. O down + 1

M. Consecutive digits in ascending order

P. D across + 7

Q. Number of minutes in four hours

Down

A. B down - 8

B. A perfect square

C. K down × 2

D. A palindrome

E. Three-fourths of Q across

I. C down × 7

J. A across - 10

K. M across - G across - 1

N. A perfect square

O. N down + 6

Symbol Sums 3

The sums of five combinations of symbols have been provided. What is the value of each individual symbol?

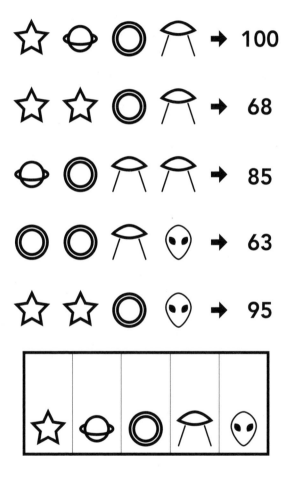

Maze 4

In this maze, you may cross under paths using tunnels where indicated by arrows.

Ringed Planet 3

Use the clues to place six words, each six letters in
length, around the planet. Words may go clockwise
or counterclockwise as needed.

Buccaneer

Paper fastener

Random knowledge

Related to a European mountain range

Restaurant necessities

Sneak peek

AND/OR 1

For each pair of clues below, find two words;
one will become the other when AND or OR are
prepended, inserted, or appended.

ST ~~AND~~ OR AGE
_____   _____

Performance platform
Place for junk

AND
OR
_____   _____

Black and white animal
Ma's partner

AND
OR
_____   _____

Furniture piece
Disinterested

AND
OR
_____   _____

Grim Adventures cartoon character
The M in OMG

AND
OR
_____   _____

Lemon-lime brew
Timid

The first puzzle has been completed to get you started!

Rearrangement 5–6

Rearrange the letters in the phrase "STUNS JAILOR" to spell the name of a group of people that ask a lot of tough questions.

Rearrange the letters in the phrase "NOSIEST ALLIES" to spell something your friends might smell if you're into aromatherapy.

Black Holes 3

Divide the grid into chunks along the guides provided so that each chunk contains one black hole, and so the digits in the chunk sum to the number in the black hole.

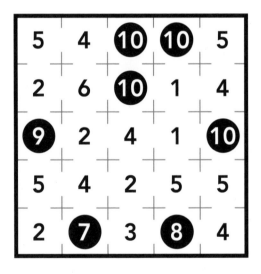

Numcross 4

Use the provided clues to fill the grid with numbers.
No entry may start with a 0.

A	B		C	D	E
F			G		
H		I			
		J		K	L
M	N			O	
P				Q	

Across

A. One-fifth of M down
C. P across + A across
F. A perfect square
G. One-half of L down
H. J across - I down + 100
J. A palindrome
M. Another palindrome
O. A perfect cube
P. L down - K down
Q. Another perfect square

Down

A. K down in reverse
B. M across - 24
C. The digits of H across
    in descending order
D. N down - 2
E. 3 × Q across
I. M across × 5
K. Consecutive digits in
    descending order
L. Consecutive digits in
    descending order
M. N down + 20
N. 3 × F across

Story Logic 3

A local venue has just finished remodeling and has lined up four stacked nights of music in a row. Use the clues to match the night, the show's sponsor, and the opener and headline act.

		Sponsor				Opener				Headline			
		Jerry's Honda	Local Cider	Taco Shack	Tropix Tan	Air Credits	Ceschi	Manchita	Prof	Aesop Rock	Dessa	Lizzo	Shredders
Day	Wednesday												
	Thursday												
	Friday												
	Saturday												
Headline	Aesop Rock												
	Dessa												
	Lizzo												
	Shredders												
Opener	Air Credits												
	Ceschi												
	Manchita												
	Prof												

Tropix Tan sponsored a show before Lizzo's show.

Air Credits did not open for Shredders or Dessa.

Lizzo, and her opening act Ceschi, were scheduled for a night before the night Local Cider sponsored.

Tropix Tan sponsored a show after the show in which Manchita performed.

Dessa's show was not sponsored by Local Cider.

Jerry's Honda sponsored the show on Friday.

Aesop Rock's show was after the show Manchita opened, but before the one that was opened by Prof.

Tetra Grid 3

Drop each of the shapes and their letters into the grid to spell ten six-letter words. Clues for the words have been provided next to the grid.

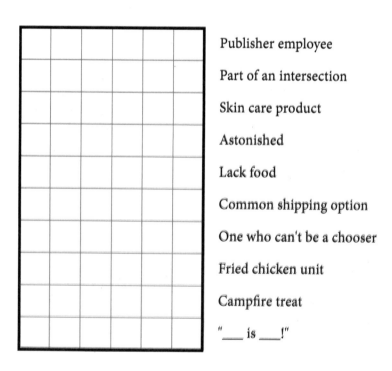

Publisher employee

Part of an intersection

Skin care product

Astonished

Lack food

Common shipping option

One who can't be a chooser

Fried chicken unit

Campfire treat

"___ is ___!"

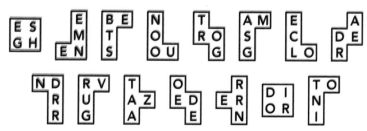

Maze 5

In this maze, you may cross under paths using
tunnels where indicated by arrows.

Cube Logic 3

Which of the four foldable patterns can be folded to make the cube displayed?

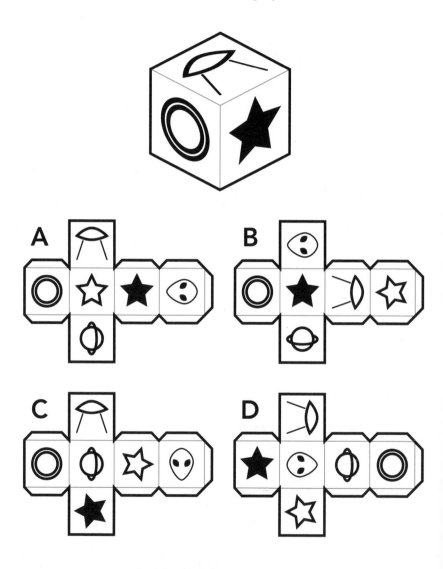

Pent Words 4

Split the grid into shapes, and use the clues provided to spell five-letter words across each row and within each shape. Shape clues include an outline, but the shape may be rotated or reflected.

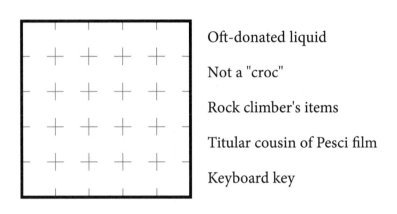

Oft-donated liquid

Not a "croc"

Rock climber's items

Titular cousin of Pesci film

Keyboard key

Bury

One-cent coin

Smells

Swell up

Group of trees

Word Sudoku 4

In the sudoku grid, enter one of each of six unique letters into each row, column, and boldly-outlined six-celled rectangle without repetition.

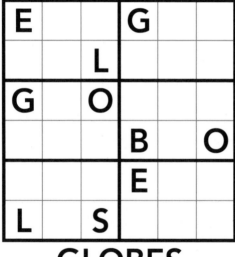

GLOBES

Black Holes 4

Divide the grid into chunks along the guides provided so that each chunk contains one black hole, and so the digits in the chunk sum to the number in the black hole.

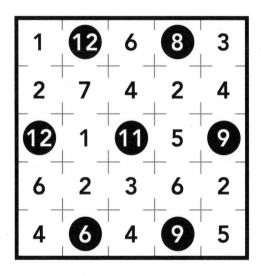

Numcross 5

Use the provided clues to fill the grid with numbers.
No entry may start with a 0.

A	B	C		D	E
F				G	
		H	I		
J	K				
L			M	N	O
P			Q		

Across

A. Consecutive digits in ascending order
D. A perfect square
F. A palindrome
G. One-third of D across
H. C down, rearranged
J. 2 × M across
L. Main N/S interstate hwy. in tornado alley
M. Consecutive digits in ascending order
P. One-fourth of O down
Q. Another perfect square

Down

A. G across - 1
B. Another perfect square
C. E down × 5
D. Another palindrome
E. B down squared
I. Another palindrome
J. A down × G across
K. 5 × N down
N. 2 × L across
O. Interstate highway along which you'd find the world's largest truckstop

Rearrangement 7–8

Rearrange the letters in the phrase "SHARPIE TIP" to spell a type of seafaring vessel one could draw with a permanent marker.

Rearrange the letters in the phrase "INK-LADEN POEM" to spell a drink about which one could wax poetic.

Symbol Sums 4

The sums of five combinations of symbols have been provided. What is the value of each individual symbol?

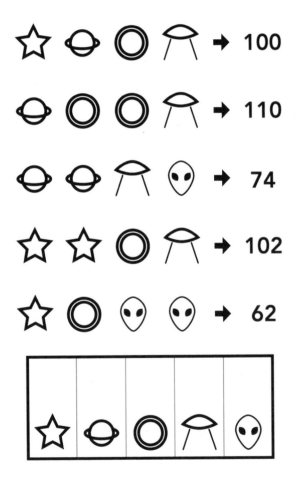

Tetra Grid 4

Drop each of the shapes and their letters into the grid to spell ten six-letter words. Clues for the words have been provided next to the grid.

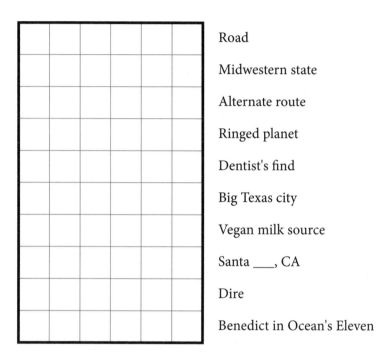

Road

Midwestern state

Alternate route

Ringed planet

Dentist's find

Big Texas city

Vegan milk source

Santa ___, CA

Dire

Benedict in Ocean's Eleven

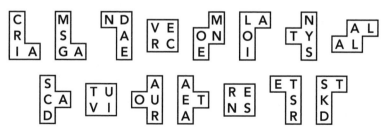

Story Logic 4

Four game developers are hard at work on their new mobile game. Use the clues provided to match each developer with their respective level and the level's theme and boss.

		Level Number				Level Boss				Level Name			
		Level 1	Level 2	Level 3	Level 4	Robot	Squirrel	Tornado	Unicorn	Aqua Zone	Big Pine Zone	Castle Zone	Desert Isle Zone
Developer	Chuck												
	Delia												
	Eddie												
	Fran												
Level Name	Aqua Zone												
	Big Pine Zone												
	Castle Zone												
	Desert Isle Zone												
Level Boss	Robot												
	Squirrel												
	Tornado												
	Unicorn												

The Squirrel boss comes in at the end of Big Pine Zone.

The Robot boss is in a level after Desert Isle Zone but before Eddie's level.

Delia was not the developer of Castle Zone.

Either Desert Isle Zone or Chuck's level was level 1.

Chuck worked on either Aqua Zone or Big Pine Zone.

Fran did not work on level 2.

Chuck's level did not feature the Robot boss.

Delia worked on the level with either the Tornado boss or the Unicorn boss.

The Squirrel boss was not the boss for level 2.

The Tornado boss is not in Castle Zone or Eddie's level.

Aqua Zone is later in the game than Big Pine Zone.

Castle Zone was not level 4.

Ringed Planet 4

Use the clues to place six words, each six letters in length, around the planet. Words may go clockwise or counterclockwise as needed.

Done over

Electrical system

Grape grower, perhaps

Place of safety

Surround

Unanchored

Cube Logic 4

Which of the four foldable patterns can be folded to make the cube displayed?

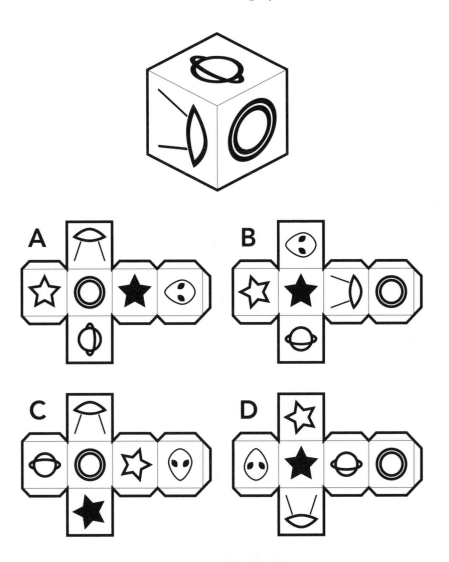

Pent Words 5

Split the grid into shapes, and use the clues provided to spell five-letter words across each row and within each shape. Shape clues include an outline, but the shape may be rotated or reflected.

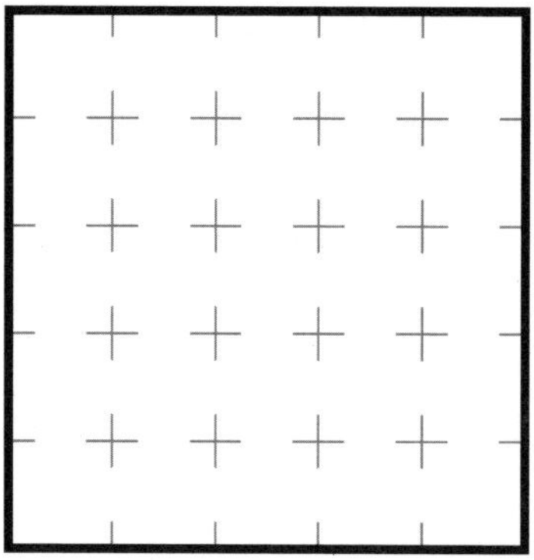

"I am ___" - ___

Blow

Tennis player Federer

Big plant life

Common door component

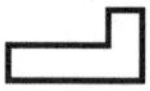

Object

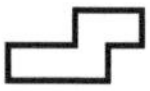

Cluster

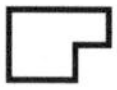

Mistake

Annoying birds

Part-time ocean-dweller

Word Sudoku 5

In the sudoku grid, enter one of each of six unique letters into each row, column, and boldly-outlined six-celled rectangle without repetition.

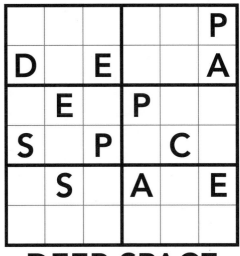

DEEP SPACE

AND/OR 2

For each pair of clues below, find two words;
one will become the other when AND or OR are
prepended, inserted, or appended.

_____	**AND** **OR** _____	Friend Directive
_____	**AND** **OR** _____	Insurance saleswoman Lava, to kids
_____	**AND** **OR** _____	Thief Routine
_____	**AND** **OR** _____	Morrison's band Two, in Mexico
_____	**AND** **OR** _____	Marked, as with an iron Reared

Numcross 6

Use the provided clues to fill the grid with numbers.
No entry may start with a 0.

A	B	■	C	D	E
F		■	G		
H		I		■	■
■		J		K	L
M	N		■	O	
P			■	Q	

Across

A. A perfect square
C. K down + 45
F. O across in reverse
G. 3 × E down
H. A palindrome
J. 3 × C across
M. A popular convenience store chain
O. Another perfect square
P. L down × 5
Q. A across - 3

Down

A. L down in reverse
B. Consecutive digits in descending order
C. The digits of J across in descending order
D. Another perfect square
E. M down - 9
I. Consecutive digits in descending order
K. One-fifth of I down
L. N down × 12
M. One-ninth of M across
N. Another perfect square

Maze 6

In this maze, you may cross under paths using
tunnels where indicated by arrows.

Symbol Sums 5

The sums of five combinations of symbols have been provided. What is the value of each individual symbol?

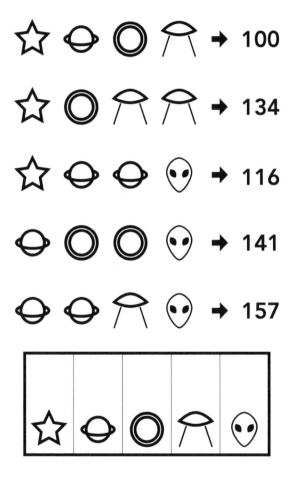

Rearrangement 9–10

Rearrange the letters in the phrase "DRY PLACE" to spell a piece of electronic equipment that should be kept dry.

Rearrange the letters in the phrase "SPOTTY BLEAR" to spell a tool that can help take care of dirty windows.

Black Holes 5

Divide the grid into chunks along the guides provided so that each chunk contains one black hole, and so the digits in the chunk sum to the number in the black hole.

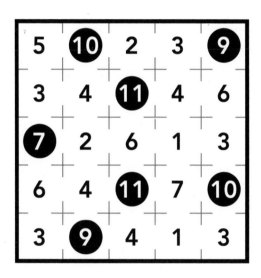

Story Logic 5

Four siblings are hard at work doing chores to
earn spending money for their upcoming summer
vacation. Use the clues to match each kid with their
age and their two chores.

		Age				Chore 1				Chore 2			
		8 Years Old	10 Years Old	12 Years Old	14 Years Old	Dishes	Lawn Mowing	Setting the Table	Walking the Dog	Laundry	Sweeping	Trash	Vacuum
Name	Junior												
	Kyle												
	Laura												
	Megan												
Chore 2	Laundry												
	Sweeping												
	Trash												
	Vacuum												
Chore 1	Dishes												
	Lawn Mowing												
	Setting the Table												
	Walking the Dog												

Junior is older than the kid that does the laundry, who themselves is older than the kid that does the dishes.

The 8-year-old kid does not vacuum the carpet or take out trash.

Kyle is older than his sister Laura.

Megan, who is 12 years old, either sets the dinner table or sweeps the floors, but does not do both.

The kid in charge of setting the table is older than the one who vacuums.

The kid that is 10 years old mows the lawn.

Cube Logic 5

Which of the four foldable patterns can be folded to make the cube displayed?

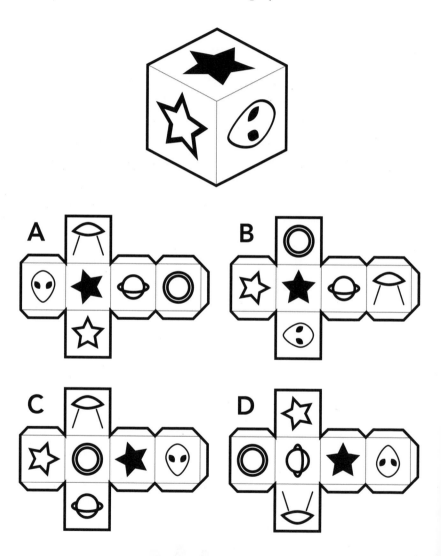

Tetra Grid 5

Drop each of the shapes and their letters into the grid to spell ten six-letter words. Clues for the words have been provided next to the grid.

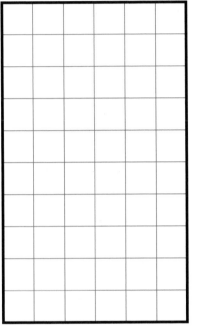

Works in progress

String instrument

The stuff of life

Like some cheeses

Assignment

Baked good

Contract or tighten

Grocery store section

Twain character Tom

Time travel destination

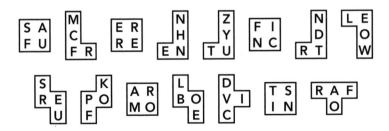

Word Sudoku 6

In the sudoku grid, enter one of each of six unique letters into each row, column, and boldly-outlined six-celled rectangle without repetition.

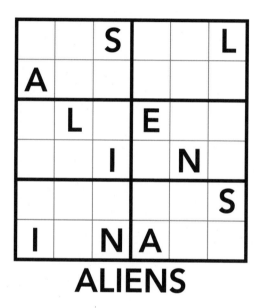

ALIENS

Pent Words 6

Split the grid into shapes, and use the clues provided to spell five-letter words across each row and within each shape. Shape clues include an outline, but the shape may be rotated or reflected.

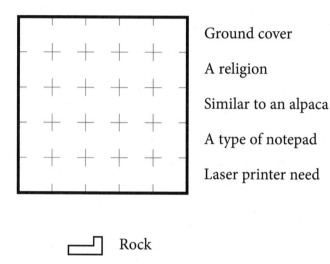

Ground cover

A religion

Similar to an alpaca

A type of notepad

Laser printer need

Rock

A type of black tea

Large house

Outdoor cooking surface

Specific rock

Symbol Sums 6

The sums of five combinations of symbols have been provided. What is the value of each individual symbol?

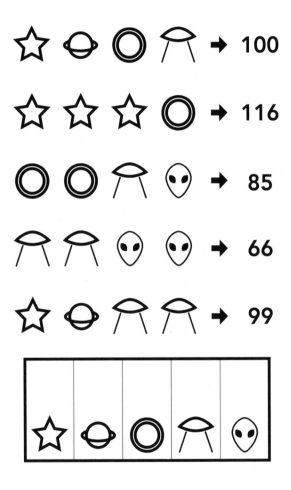

Rearrangement 11–12

Rearrange the letters in the phrase "CAPTAIN'S TOES" to spell a place where one might accidentally bump into crewmates while floating.

Rearrange the letters in the phrase "TWOFER HAUL" to spell a good item for a professional baker to score on sale.

Numcross 7

Use the provided clues to fill the grid with numbers.
No entry may start with a 0.

A	B		C	D	E		F	G	H
I			J				K		
L		M				N			
		O		P	Q				
R	S			T			U	V	W
X				Y			Z		
		AA			BB				
CC	DD	EE			FF		GG	HH	
II			JJ	KK			LL		
MM			NN				OO		

Across

A. N down + 1
C. One-third of GG down
F. AA down squared
I. O across / N across
J. HH down + 8
K. A perfect square
L. X across × N down
N. Consecutive digits in ascending order
O. Contains every even digit (0, 2, 4, 6, 8)
R. Consecutive digits in descending order
T. S down + 1
U. Another perfect square
X. Digits that sum to 17
Y. A across × 3
Z. V down × N down
AA. Contains every odd digit (1, 3, 5, 7, 9)
CC. P down in reverse
FF. U down - J across
II. 2 × F across
JJ. V down × OO across
LL. Another perfect square
MM. I across squared
NN. D down × 6
OO. AA across / U across

Down

A. Consecutive digits in ascending order
B. One-half of F down
C. 3 × X across
D. KK down + AA down
E. W down - OO across
F. A palindrome
G. GG down - I across
H. U across - A across
M. Another palindrome
N. One-half of I across
P. U down + D down
Q. Digits that sum to 21
R. S down + 7
S. Another perfect square
U. U across × N down
V. Another perfect square
W. 2 × V down
AA. Another perfect square
BB. Consecutive digits in descending order
CC. B down × 9
DD. OO across × N down
EE. AA down × I across
GG. Consecutive digits in descending order
HH. Another palindrome
JJ. V down × 3
KK. JJ down - 2

Tetra Grid 6

Drop each of the shapes and their letters into the
grid to spell ten six-letter words. Clues for the words
have been provided next to the grid.

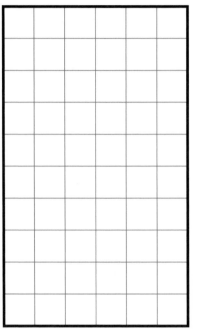

Quesadilla star

Essential

Fashionable

All set

Growths

Hospital attire

More than twice

Paddock or pen

E.g. briefly, loudly

Headphone purpose

Black Holes 6

Divide the grid into chunks along the guides provided so that each chunk contains one black hole, and so the digits in the chunk sum to the number in the black hole.

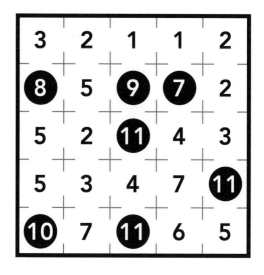

Word Sudoku 7

In the sudoku grid, enter one of each of six unique letters into each row, column, and boldly-outlined six-celled rectangle without repetition.

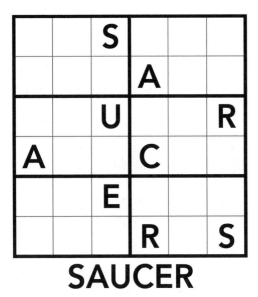

Ringed Planet 5

Use the clues to place six words, each six letters in
length, around the planet. Words may go clockwise
or counterclockwise as needed.

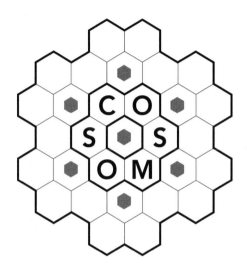

Disaster

Like some networks

Name-brand grease

Olympic games haul

Pointy-hatted garden dwellers

Potentially deadly substance

Pent Words 7

Split the grid into shapes, and use the clues provided
to spell five-letter words across each row and within
each shape. Shape clues include an outline, but the
shape may be rotated or reflected.

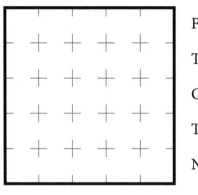

Freddie Mercury's band

Type of beer

Coal worker

Tied, as with shoes

Number after 8, by radio

Eatery

Italian city

Mission

One-sixteenth of a pound

Opposite of exit

Word Sudoku 8

In the sudoku grid, enter one of each of six unique letters into each row, column, and boldly-outlined six-celled rectangle without repetition.

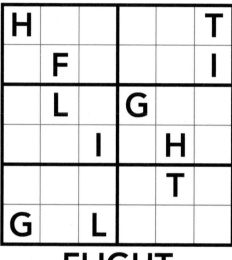

FLIGHT

Story Logic 6

Doh! In a total brain misfire, you've forgotten to label your planters this year. Use the clues to match the planter with what you put in it and which plant food and water it needs.

		Plant				Food				Water			
		Basil	Chives	Kale	Peppers	Earthly Choice	Greene Thumb	Natural Selection	Red Label	1 Cup	2 Cups	3 Cups	4 Cups
Planter	Green												
	Tan												
	Terra Cotta												
	Window Box												
Water	1 Cup												
	2 Cups												
	3 Cups												
	4 Cups												
Food	Earthly Choice												
	Greene Thumb												
	Natural Selection												
	Red Label												

The plants in the window box planter do not need to be fed with Earthly Choice or Red Label plant food.

The pepper plants require twice as much water as the plants in the tan planter.

Chives are not being grown in the window box planter or the green planter.

Kale does not need four cups of water.

The plant fed Earthly Choice needs more water than the one fed Greene Thumb, but less than the kale plant.

The terra cotta planter needs twice as much water as the one fed Earthly Choice.

Basil is planted either in the terra cotta planter or the one fed Natural Selection.

Symbol Sums 7

The sums of five combinations of symbols have been provided. What is the value of each individual symbol?

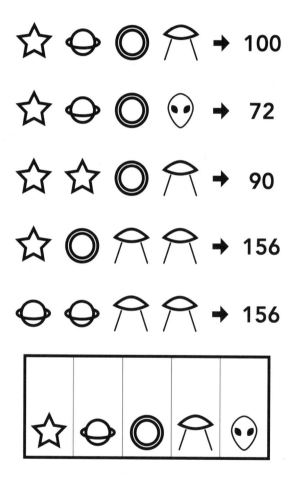

Maze 7

In this maze, you may cross under paths using tunnels where indicated by arrows.

Rearrangement 13–14

Rearrange the letters in the phrase "ABSURDLY TAKEN" to spell something only a real jerk would steal from a laundromat.

Rearrange the letters in the phrase "NO TSUNAMI" to spell a place that definitely counts as high ground.

AND/OR 3

For each pair of clues below, find two words;
one will become the other when AND or OR are
prepended, inserted, or appended.

_____	**AND** **OR** _____	Place to sleep Striped
_____	**AND** **OR** _____	West coast state abbr. Reef dweller
_____	**AND** **OR** _____	Female pronoun Where land meets water
_____	**AND** **OR** _____	Movie effects Breed of dog
_____	**AND** **OR** _____	Spirits A gender

Cube Logic 6

Which of the four foldable patterns can be folded to make the cube displayed?

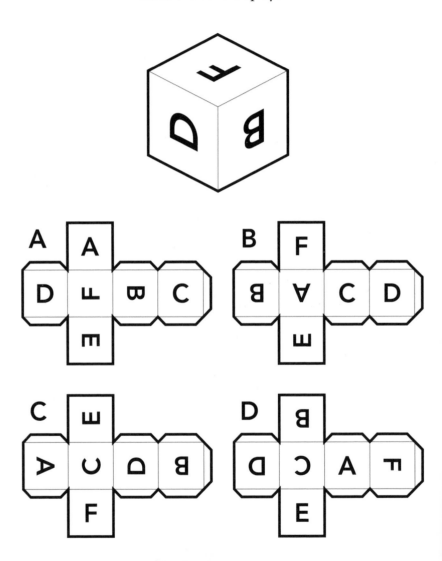

Symbol Sums 8

The sums of five combinations of symbols have been provided. What is the value of each individual symbol?

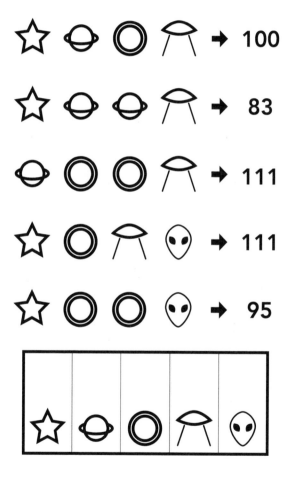

Black Holes 7

Divide the grid into chunks along the guides
provided so that each chunk contains one black
hole, and so the digits in the chunk sum to the
number in the black hole.

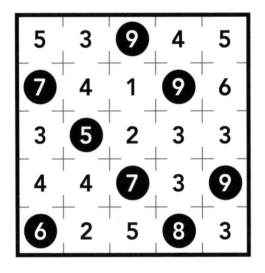

Pent Words 8

Split the grid into shapes, and use the clues provided to spell five-letter words across each row and within each shape. Shape clues include an outline, but the shape may be rotated or reflected.

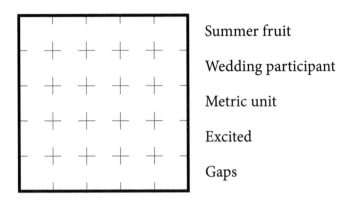

Summer fruit

Wedding participant

Metric unit

Excited

Gaps

Stay away

Solitary person

Some Monopoly game cards

Floating craft

Type of badges

Black Holes 8

Divide the grid into chunks along the guides provided so that each chunk contains one black hole, and so the digits in the chunk sum to the number in the black hole.

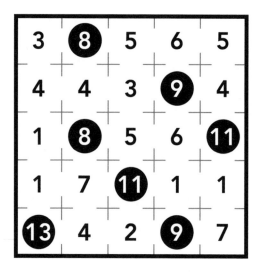

Rearrangement 15–16

Rearrange the letters in the phrase "RANCID SOUL" to spell the kind of weather that an emo teenager might enjoy.

Rearrange the letters in the phrase "OVEREAT TONS" to spell a potentially game-changing kitchen appliance.

Numcross 8

Use the provided clues to fill the grid with numbers.
No entry may start with a 0.

A	B	C	D		E	F		G	H
I					J		K		
		L		M		N			
O	P		Q		R			S	T
U		V		W			X		
Y			Z				AA		
BB			CC			DD		EE	
		FF			GG		HH		
II	JJ			KK		LL		MM	NN
OO			PP			QQ			

Across

A. A palindrome
E. A perfect square
G. Another perfect square
I. (10 × HH down) + 2
J. R down + QQ across
L. (2 × HH down) - 1
N. One-half of FF across
O. JJ down + 1
Q. BB across squared
S. O across + 3
U. 8 × V down
W. Contains one of each even digit (0, 2, 4, 6, 8)
Y. G down converted from base 10 to binary
AA. (2 × GG across) + 8
BB. 2 × E across
CC. 2 × Q across
EE. X down + 4
FF. EE across + 2
GG. HH down + C down
II. Z down + L across
LL. I across + BB across
OO. A down - 4
PP. II down × 4
QQ. 2 × S down

Down

A. B down + II down
B. II down - 1
C. A palindrome
D. The sum of its digits is the same as T down's.
E. E across - 3
F. 2 × J across
G. G across - 2
H. G down × 2
K. E across - 1
M. Famous Beverly Hills zip code and TV show
O. GG across × E down
P. CC across in reverse
R. Another palindrome
S. 2 × T down
T. The sum of its digits is the same as D down's
V. Another perfect square
X. A perfect cube
Z. QQ across × 2
DD. I across × 8
FF. EE across + 4
HH. Another perfect square
II. PP across - MM down
JJ. Another perfect cube
KK. 2 × OO across
MM. Forms a run with S acr., BB acr., KK dn, N acr.
NN. The answer to the ultimate question

Tetra Grid 7A

Drop each of the shapes and their letters into the grid to spell ten six-letter words. Clues for the words have been provided next to the grid.

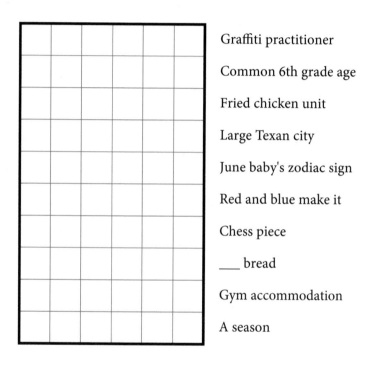

Graffiti practitioner

Common 6th grade age

Fried chicken unit

Large Texan city

June baby's zodiac sign

Red and blue make it

Chess piece

___ bread

Gym accommodation

A season

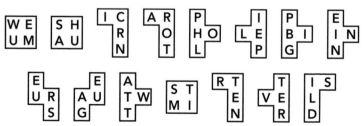

Tetra Grid 7B

Drop each of the shapes and their letters into the grid to spell ten six-letter words. Clues for the words have been provided next to the grid.

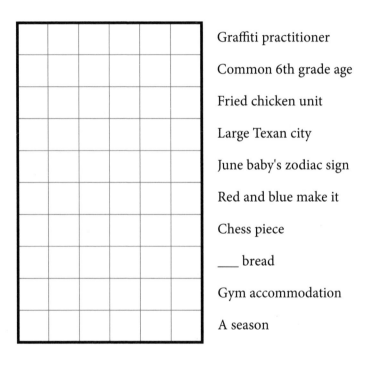

Graffiti practitioner

Common 6th grade age

Fried chicken unit

Large Texan city

June baby's zodiac sign

Red and blue make it

Chess piece

___ bread

Gym accommodation

A season

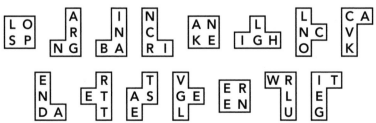

Black Holes 9

Divide the grid into chunks along the guides provided so that each chunk contains one black hole, and so the digits in the chunk sum to the number in the black hole.

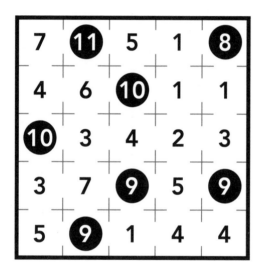

Cube Logic 7

Which of the four foldable patterns can be folded to make the cube displayed?

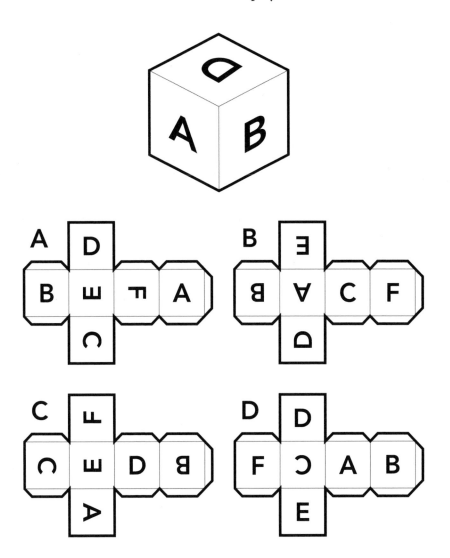

Maze 8

In this maze, you may cross under paths using tunnels where indicated by arrows.

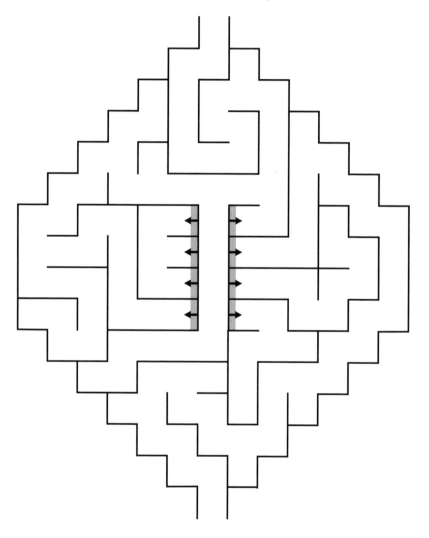

Ringed Planet 6

Use the clues to place six words, each six letters in length, around the planet. Words may go clockwise or counterclockwise as needed.

Egyptian king

Cluster

Medical caretakers

Place in custody

Underground train system

Varying

Tetra Grid 8

Drop each of the shapes and their letters into the grid to spell ten six-letter words. Clues for the words have been provided next to the grid.

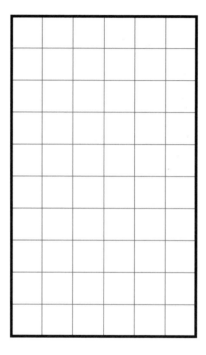

Socket

Comedian Dangerfield

City in New York

The great outdoors

Hot spice

Mercury's elemental number

Part of a shirt

Round but not circular

Warning sign word

E.g. Gala and Granny Smith

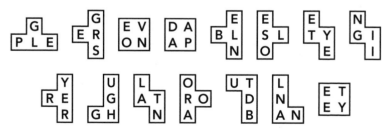

Black Holes 10

Divide the grid into chunks along the guides
provided so that each chunk contains one black
hole, and so the digits in the chunk sum to the
number in the black hole.

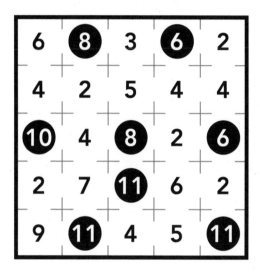

Cube Logic 8

Which of the four foldable patterns can be folded to make the cube displayed?

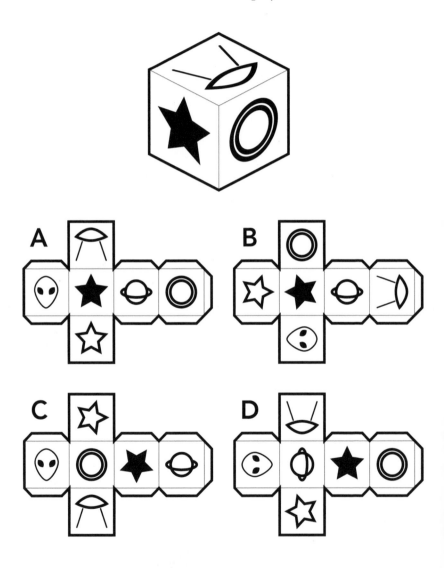

Black Holes 11

Divide the grid into chunks along the guides provided so that each chunk contains one black hole, and so the digits in the chunk sum to the number in the black hole.

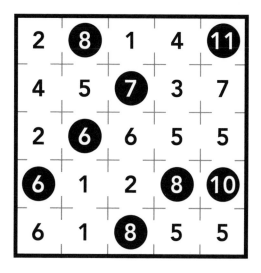

Rearrangement 17–18

Rearrange the letters in the phrase "AGED GALS" to spell a kind of sandwich that kids these days aren't really into.

Rearrange the letters in the phrase "VOICE RUMORS" to spell the name of a singer that would cause quite a stir were he to lose his voice.

Black Holes 12

Divide the grid into chunks along the guides provided so that each chunk contains one black hole, and so the digits in the chunk sum to the number in the black hole.

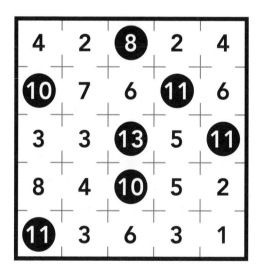

Word Sudoku 9

In the sudoku grid, enter one of each of six unique letters into each row, column, and boldly-outlined six-celled rectangle without repetition.

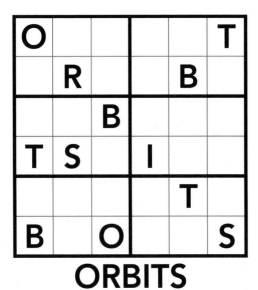

ORBITS

Answer Keys

AND/OR 1:   St(or)age, P(and)a, B(or)ed, M(and)y, Sh(and)y
2:   M(and)ate, Flo(or), B(and)it, Do(or)s, Br(and)ed
3:   B(and)ed, C(or)al, Sh(or)e, C(or)gi, M(or)ale

Black Holes 1

Black Holes 2

Black Holes 3

Black Holes 4

Black Holes 5

Black Holes 6

Black Holes 7

Black Holes 8

Black Holes 9

Black Holes 10

Black Holes 11

Black Holes 12

Cube Logic 1: Pattern C   5: Pattern B
2: Pattern A   6: Pattern D
3: Pattern D   7: Pattern A
4: Pattern D   8: Pattern C

Maze 1

Maze 2

Maze 3

Maze 4

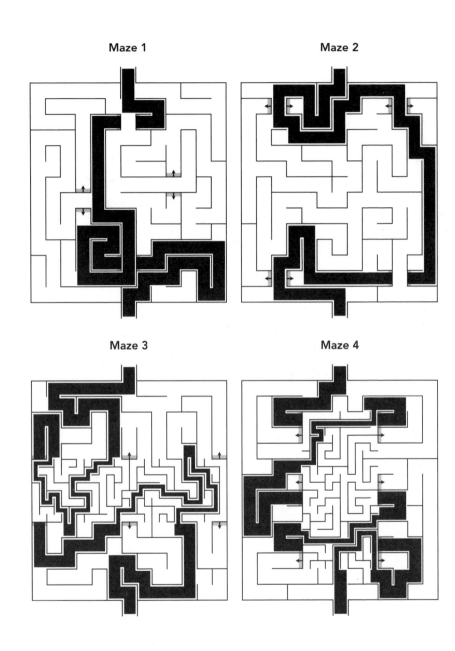

Maze 5

Maze 6

Maze 7

Maze 8

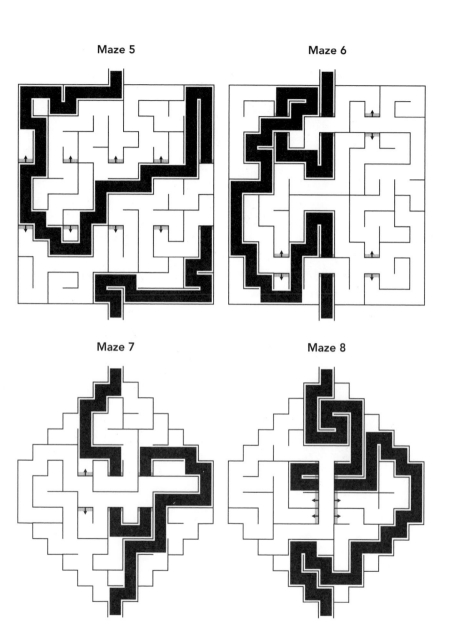

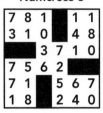

Numcross 1

```
3 6 9 █ 2 6
7 1 7 █ 3 1
█ █ 1 9 9 9
1 9 7 9 █ █
2 0 █ 9 6 1
1 0 █ 1 2 3
```

Numcross 2

```
1 6 █ 9 4 9
1 3 █ 2 8 6
2 0 1 7 █ █
█ █ 6 0 5 1
2 8 0 █ 4 9
2 0 0 █ 3 2
```

Numcross 3

```
7 8 1 █ 1 1
3 1 0 █ 4 8
█ █ 3 7 1 0
7 5 6 2 █ █
7 1 █ 5 6 7
1 8 █ 2 4 0
```

Numcross 4

```
1 9 █ 5 7 4
2 5 █ 4 3 8
3 5 4 3 █ █
█ █ 8 3 3 8
9 7 9 █ 2 7
5 5 5 █ 1 6
```

Numcross 5

```
1 2 3 █ 3 6
1 5 1 █ 1 2
█ █ 2 1 3 5
1 3 5 6 █ █
3 5 █ 6 7 8
2 0 █ 1 0 0
```

Numcross 6

```
2 5 █ 6 8 7
9 4 █ 2 1 0
1 3 3 1 █ █
█ █ 2 0 6 1
7 1 1 █ 4 9
9 6 0 █ 2 2
```

Numcross 7

```
1 1 █ 1 8 1 █ 2 5 6
2 0 █ 1 9 9 █ 1 2 1
3 6 8 0 █ █ 1 2 3 4
█ █ 2 4 6 8 0 █ █ █
4 3 2 █ 3 7 █ 6 2 5
3 6 8 █ 3 3 █ 2 5 0
█ █ █ 1 9 3 7 5 █ █
9 3 3 6 █ █ 6 0 5 1
5 1 2 █ 7 7 5 █ 4 9
4 0 0 █ 5 3 4 █ 3 1
```

Numcross 8

```
2 1 1 2 █ 1 6 █ 4 9
1 0 0 2 █ 3 0 1 7 4
█ █ 1 9 9 █ 3 5 █ █
2 8 █ 1 0 2 4 █ 3 1
6 4 8 █ 2 4 8 6 0 5
1 0 1 1 1 1 █ 4 1 0
3 2 █ 2 0 4 8 █ 6 8
█ █ 7 0 █ 2 0 1 █ █
1 2 2 6 3 █ 1 0 3 4
1 7 █ 4 4 █ 6 0 3 2
```

Pent Words 1

```
P H O N E
S T O V E
C L E A R
A C O R N
R Y D E R
```

Pent Words 2

```
C U B A N
M I N A J
T A N G O
H O T E L
E R I C K
```

Pent Words 3

```
A G R E E
M I D A S
S H A D E
W H A L E
E R E C T
```

Pent Words 4

```
B L O O D
G A T O R
R O P E S
V I N N Y
E N T E R
```

Pent Words 5

```
G R O O T
E R U P T
R O G E R
T R E E S
H I N G E
```

Pent Words 6

```
G R A S S
I S L A M
L L A M A
S T E N O
T O N E R
```

Pent Words 7

```
Q U E E N
S T O U T
M I N E R
L A C E D
N I N E R
```

Pent Words 8

```
M E L O N
B R I D E
L I T E R
A M P E D
V O I D S
```

Rearrangement

1:	Sliced Bread	10:	Spray Bottle
2:	Sonic the Hedgehog	11:	Space Station
3:	Kale Chips	12:	Wheat Flour
4:	Four-Egg Omelet	13:	Laundry Basket
5:	Journalists	14:	Mountains
6:	Essential Oils	15:	Rain clouds
7:	Pirate Ship	16:	Toaster Oven
8:	Pink Lemonade	17:	Egg Salad
9:	CD Player	18:	Rivers Cuomo

Ringed Planet 1

Ringed Planet 2

Ringed Planet 3

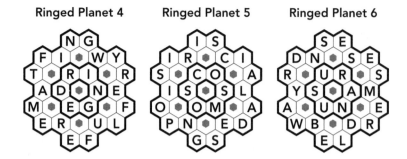

Ringed Planet 4   **Ringed Planet 5**   **Ringed Planet 6**

Story Logic 1   Miley ordered a small eclair coffee which cost $2.25.

Nupur ordered a medium donut shop blend which cost $1.25.

Ozie ordered an extra large fudge coffee which cost $3.25.

Paige ordered a large caramel coffee drink which cost $1.75.

Story Logic 2   Booth 103 is Knasty Knits where $10 was spent.

Booth 104 is Sandworks where $5 was spent.

Booth 105 is Brooks Leather where $20 was spent.

Booth 106 is Misremembered Things where $40 was spent.

Booth 107 is Lee's Lotions where $15 was spent.

Booth 108 is Chimes by Linda where $30 was spent.

Story Logic 3   Wednesday, Dessa w/ Manchita, sponsored by Taco Shack

Thursday, Aesop Rock w/ Air Credits, sponsored by Tropix Tan

Friday, Lizzo w/ Ceschi, sponsored by Jerry's Honda

Saturday, Shredders w/ Prof, sponsored by Local Cider

Story Logic 4   Level 1: Big Pine Zone by Chuck with Squirrel boss

Level 2: Desert Island Zone by Delia with Tornado boss

Level 3: Castle Run Zone by Fran with Robot boss

Level 4: Aqua Zone by Eddie with Unicorn boss

Story Logic 5 Junior, age 14, walks the dog and takes out the trash.
Kyle, age 10, mows the lawn and vacuums the carpet.
Laura, age 8, washes dishes and sweeps the floor.
Megan, age 12, sets the dinner table and washes the laundry.

Story Logic 6 Green planter: pepper plants, 2 cups water, Earthly Choice
Tan planter: chives, 1 cup water, Greene Thumb
Terra Cotta planter: basil plants, 4 cups water, Red Label
Window box: kale, 3 cups water, Natural Selection

Symbol Sums 1

17	8	33	42	12

Symbol Sums 2

32	11	21	36	9

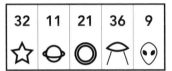

Symbol Sums 3

25	57	8	10	37

Symbol Sums 4

20	18	30	32	6

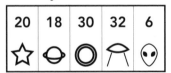

Symbol Sums 5

9	16	25	50	75

Symbol Sums 6

30	19	26	25	8

Symbol Sums 7

1	11	21	67	39

Symbol Sums 8

17	11	28	44	22

Tetra Grid 1

```
C O W A R D
S L O W L Y
G A R A G E
V I K I N G
T R I P O D
V O T E R S
L E G E N D
B O U N C E
P O R O U S
S I L E N T
```

Tetra Grid 2

```
C H E R R Y
S U M M E R
F R I D A Y
G A R L I C
R E W A R D
A F R A I D
T H R I L L
W E I G H T
P E N C I L
R E M O T E
```

Tetra Grid 3

```
E D I T O R
C O R N E R
L O T I O N
A M A Z E D
S T A R V E
G R O U N D
B E G G A R
T E N D E R
S M O R E S
E N O U G H
```

Tetra Grid 4

```
S T R E E T
K A N S A S
D E T O U R
S A T U R N
C A V I T Y
D A L L A S
A L M O N D
M O N I C A
S E V E R E
G A R C I A
```

Tetra Grid 5

```
D R A F T S
V I O L I N
C A R B O N
S M O K E D
R E P O R T
M U F F I N
C L E N C H
F R O Z E N
S A W Y E R
F U T U R E
```

Tetra Grid 6

```
C H E E S E
S T A P L E
T R E N D Y
G O L D E N
P O L Y P S
S C R U B S
T H R I C E
C O R R A L
A D V E R B
L I S T E N
```

Tetra Grid 7 A

```
A R T I S T
T W E L V E
T E N D E R
A U S T I N
G E M I N I
P U R P L E
B I S H O P
G A R L I C
S H O W E R
A U T U M N
```

Tetra Grid 7 B

```
W R I T E R
E L E V E N
N U G G E T
D A L L A S
C A N C E R
V I O L E T
K N I G H T
B A N A N A
L O C K E R
S P R I N G
```

Tetra Grid 8

```
O U T L E T
R O D N E Y
A L B A N Y
N A T U R E
G I N G E R
E I G H T Y
S L E E V E
O B L O N G
D A N G E R
A P P L E S
```

Word Sudoku 1

N	A	U	E	B	L
B	E	L	A	U	N
U	N	B	L	A	E
A	L	E	U	N	B
E	B	A	N	L	U
L	U	N	B	E	A

Word Sudoku 2

A	V	Y	E	G	O
G	E	O	V	Y	A
E	O	V	Y	A	G
Y	G	A	O	V	E
V	A	E	G	O	Y
O	Y	G	A	E	V

Word Sudoku 3

E	C	S	T	M	O
M	O	T	C	E	S
C	E	M	S	O	T
S	T	O	E	C	M
O	S	C	M	T	E
T	M	E	O	S	C

Word Sudoku 4

E	S	B	G	O	L
O	G	L	S	E	B
G	B	O	L	S	E
S	L	E	B	G	O
B	O	G	E	L	S
L	E	S	O	B	G

Word Sudoku 5

A	C	S	D	E	P
D	P	E	C	S	A
C	E	D	P	A	S
S	A	P	E	C	D
P	S	C	A	D	E
E	D	A	S	P	C

Word Sudoku 6

E	N	S	I	A	L
A	I	L	S	E	N
N	L	A	E	S	I
S	E	I	L	N	A
L	A	E	N	I	S
I	S	N	A	L	E

Word Sudoku 7

U	A	S	E	R	C
R	E	C	A	S	U
E	C	U	S	A	R
A	S	R	C	U	E
S	R	E	U	C	A
C	U	A	R	E	S

Word Sudoku 8

H	I	G	F	L	T
L	F	T	H	G	I
T	L	H	G	I	F
F	G	I	T	H	L
I	H	F	L	T	G
G	T	L	I	F	H

Word Sudoku 9

O	B	I	S	R	T
S	R	T	O	B	I
I	O	B	T	S	R
T	S	R	I	O	B
R	I	S	B	T	O
B	T	O	R	I	S

Thanks for solving!

Exercise Your Mind at American Mensa

At American Mensa, we love puzzles. In fact, we have events—large and small—centered around games and puzzles.

Of course, at 55,000 members and growing, we're much more than that, with members aged 2 to 102 and from all walks of life. Our one shared trait might be one you share, too: high intelligence, measured in the top 2 percent of the general public in a standardized test.

Get-togethers with other Mensans—from small pizza nights up to larger events like our annual Mind Games—are always stimulating and fun. Roughly 130 Special Interest Groups (we call them SIGs) offer the best of the real and virtual worlds. Highlighting the Mensa newsstand is our award-winning magazine, *Mensa Bulletin*, which stimulates the curious mind with unique features that add perspective to our fast-paced world.

And then there are the practical benefits of membership, such as exclusive offers through our partners and member discounts on magazine subscriptions, online shopping, and financial services.

Find out how to qualify or take our practice test at americanmensa.org/join.